CANINE LIBRARY

C000115375

PEDIGREE DOGS IN ᴄᴏʟᴏᴜʀ

BOOK FOUR

UTILITY GROUP

Official Standards
and
Colour Illustrations

OTHER TITLES AVAILABLE
OR IN PREPARATION

20th Century Bulldog — by Marjorie Barnard
The Kennelgarth Scottish Terrier Book — by Betty Penn-Bull
The Bulldog — A Monograph by Edgar Farman
Keeshond of the World — by Margo Emerson
Staffordshire Bull Terrier in History and Sport — by Mike Homan
The Bullmastiff — by Clifford L.B. Hubbard
The Butterfly Dog — by Clarice Waud and Pat Chalice (limp)
The German Shepherd Dog — by Joyce Ixer
The Dalmation — by Clifford L.B. Hubbard
Toy Dogs — A Comprehensive Guide to Toy Dogs (HB) C. Waud
    and Mark Hutchings
Concise Guide to Dog Showing — by Paddy Petch (limp)
The Dog Book — by Betty Penn-Bull (limp)
Small Dog Obedience Training — by Mrs. R.A. Foreman (limp)
Bird Dogs of the World — Stanley .W.C. Smith

PEDIGREE DOGS IN COLOUR

BOOK FOUR

UTILITY GROUP

Roy Hodrien

Official Standards

*Colour Illustrations by
the Author*

NIMROD PRESS LTD

Dedicated to the memory of
Nan and Charlie

© Roy Hodrien and Nimrod Press Ltd., 1990

This book is copyright under the Berne Convention. All rights are reserved. Apart from any fair dealing for the purposes of private study, research, criticism or review, as permitted under the Copyright Act, 1956, no part of this publication may be reproduced, stored in a retrieval system, or transmitted in any form or by any means, electronic, electrical, chemical, mechanical, optical, photocopying, recording or otherwise, without the prior written permission of the copyright owner. Enquiries should be addressed to the publishers.

First Published in 1990

Pedigree Dogs in Colour   ISBN 1 85259 094 7

Book One – Hounds   ISBN 1 85259 205 2
Book Two – Gundogs   ISBN 1 85259 206 0
Book Three – Terriers   ISBN 1 85259 207 9
Book Four – Utility Group   ISBN 1 85259 208 7
Book Five – Working Group ISBN 1 85259 209 5
Book Six – Toy Group   ISBN 1 85259 210 9

NIMROD PRESS LTD
15 The Maltings
Turk Street
Alton, Hants, GU34 1DL

Produced by Jamesway Graphics
Middleton, Manchester

Printed in England

CONTENTS

BOOK THREE – **TERRIERS**

BOOK FOUR – **UTILITY GROUP**

BOOK FIVE – **WORKING GROUP**

BOOK SIX – **TOY GROUP**

ACKNOWLEDGEMENTS

My thanks are offered to all those who assisted with this book. In particular I acknowledge the role of the British Kennel Club who gave permission for the *Official Standards* to be reproduced. The American Club also kindly allowed me to quote from their *Standards* showing the main variations from the British Standards.

ROY HODRIEN

PEDIGREE DOGS IN COLOUR

BOOK FOUR
UTILITY GROUP

This is Book Four in a volume consisting of six books each dealing with a main group of dogs. The page numbering follows that used in the main volume.

Boston Terrier

BOSTON TERRIER

This good-natured, attractive little dog was developed in the U.S.A. from English breeds. As the face would suggest, one of these breeds was the Bulldog and the athletic lines of the torso and legs are derived from terrier stock. This early breeding work took place in Boston, Massachusetts in the mid-nineteenth century, hence the naming of the breed. He became a popular dog almost immediately and show appearances inevitably followed. When enthusiasts formed a breed club, they had wanted to call their dogs American Bull Terriers but this was opposed by Bull Terrier breeders and the present name was eventually settled upon.

At one time the Boston Terrier was the most popular dog in the U.S.A., and whilst not enjoying quite such success now, he is still very much an American favourite. He is also far from rare in Britain, although devotees of the breed are surprised that his following is not even larger here. He is certainly an appealing breed, combining all the manageability and charm of a small dog with the toughness and courage of a much larger breed. He guards his master's property very keenly and is loyal and affectionate with the whole family.

If feeding is kept at a sensible level, the Boston Terrier's exercise needs are not too great, but he will enjoy regular walks and occasional runs in the open.

KEY TO CHARACTER	
INTELLIGENCE	****
TEMPERAMENT	*****
EASE OF COAT CARE	*****
SUITABILITY FOR SMALL DWELLING	*****
***** (5) = VERY GOOD	

BRITISH KENNEL CLUB STANDARD

BOSTON TERRIER

CHARACTERISTICS. — A proportionate combination of "Colour" and "Ideal Markings" is a particularly distinctive feature of a representative specimen. A dog with a preponderance of white on body or without the proper proportion of brindle and white on head is at a disadvantage. The ideal "Boston Terrier Expression" as indicating "a high degree of intelligence" is also an important characteristic of the breed. "Colour and Markings" and "Expression" should be given particular consideration in determining the relative value of "General Appearance" to other points.

GENERAL APPEARANCE. — The general appearance of the Boston Terrier should be that of a lively, highly intelligent, smooth-coated, short-headed, compactly built, short-tailed, well balanced dog of medium size, of brindle colour and evenly marked with white. The head should indicate a high degree of intelligence and should be in proportion to the size of the dog; the body rather short and well knit; the limbs strong and neatly turned; tail short and no feature to be so prominent that the dog appears badly proportioned. The dog should convey an impression of determination, strength and activity, with style of a high order; carriage easy and graceful. The gait of the Boston Terrier is that of a sure-footed straight-gaited dog, forelegs and hindlegs moving straight ahead in time with perfect rhythm, each step indicating grace and power.

Head and Skull. — Skull square, flat on top, free from wrinkles; cheeks flat; brow abrupt, stop well defined. Muzzle short, square, wide and deep, and in proportion to the skull; free form wrinkles; shorter in length than in width and depth, not exceeding in length approximately one-third of length of skull; width and depth carried out well to end; the muzzle from stop to end of nose on a line parallel to the top of the skull; nose black and wide with well-defined line between nostrils. The jaws broad and square. The chops of good depth but not pendulous, completely covering the teeth when mouth is closed.

Eyes. — Wide apart, large and round, dark in colour, expression alert but kind and intelligent. The eyes should set square in the skull, and the outside corners should be on a line with the cheeks as viewed from the front.

Ears. — Carried ererct; small and thin; situated as near corner of skull as possible.

Mouth. — Teeth short and regular, bite even, or sufficiently undershot to square muzzle.

Neck. — Of fair length, slightly arched and carrying the head gracefully; neatly set into the shoulders.

Forequarters. — Legs set moderately wide apart and on a line with the point of the shoulders; straight in bone and well muscled; pasterns short and strong. Elbows standing neither in nor out.

Body. — Deep with good width of chest; shoulders sloping, back short; ribs deep and well sprung, carried well back to loins; loins short and muscular; rump curving slightly to set-on of tail; flank very slightly cut up. The body should appear short but not chunky.

Hindquarters. — Legs set true, bent at stifles, short from hocks to feet; hocks turning neither in nor out; thighs strong and well muscled.

Feet. — Round, small and compact, and turned neither in nor out; toes well arched.

Tail. — Set-on low; short, fine and tapering; straight or screw; devoid of fringes or coarse hair, and not carried above horizontal.

Coat. — Short, smooth, bright and fine in texture.

Colour. — Brindle with white markings; brindle must show throughout the body distinctly; black and white markings are permissible, but brindles with white markings are preferred. (Ideal colour shall be one in which the brindle colouring is evenly distributed throughout the body). Ideal markings: white muzzle, even white blaze over head, collar, breast, part or whole of forelegs, and hind legs below hocks.

Weight and Size. — Weight should not exceed 11.4 kg (25 lbs) divided by classes as follows: Lightweight, under 6.8 kg (15 lbs); Middleweight, 6.8 kg (15 lbs) and under 9.1 kg (20 lbs); Heavyweight, 9.1 kg (20 lbs) and under 11.4 kg (25 lbs).

Faults. — Solid black, black and tan; liver or mouse colour; Dudley nose; docked tail. Skull "domed" or inclined; furrowed by a medial line; skull too long for breadth, or vice versa; stop too shallow; brow and skull too slanting. Eyes small or sunken; too prominent; light colour or wall eye; showing too much white or haw. Muzzle wedge-shaped or lacking depth; down faced; too much cut out below the eyes; pinched or wide nostrils; butterfly nose; protruding teeth; weak lower jaw; showing "turn-up". Ears poorly carried or in size out of proportion to the head. Neck: ewe-necked; throaty, short or thick. Body: flat sides; narrow chest; long or slack loins; roach back; sway back; too much cut-up in flank. Loose shoulders or elbows; hind legs too straight at stifles; hocks too prominent; long or weak pasterns; splay feet. A long or gaily carried tail; extremely gnarled or curled against body. (Note — The preferred tail should not exceed in length approximately half the distance from the set-on to hock). Colour and markings: all white; absence of white markings; preponderance of white on body; without the proper proportion of brindle and white on head; or any variations detracting from the general appearance. Coat: long or coarse; lacking lustre.

Note. — Male animals should have two apparently normal testicles fully descended into the scrotum.

MAIN AMERICAN KENNEL CLUB VARIATION TO STANDARD FOR THE BOSTON TERRIER —

Ears. — Carried erect, either cropped to conform to the shape of the head, or natural bat, situated as near the corners of skull as possible.

BOSTON TERRIER REGISTRATIONS 1981 — 87 INCLUSIVE

```
1981 —  93
1982 —  93
1983 —  94
1984 —  75
1985 — 101
1986 — 102
1987 — 112
```

YET TO WIN CRUFTS BEST-IN-SHOW.

BULLDOG

The Bulldog is a direct descendant of the Molossian Dog of ancient Greece, a type of dog used for ceremonial fighting against men and various kinds of beast. It is most probable that these huge vicious dogs were the common ancestors for all short faced heavily built dogs, the Mastiff and Bullmastiff being others which fall into this category.

The Bulldog had developed into something like his present form by the thirteenth century. He was then widely used for the grisly pastime of bull baiting. This would involve a bull being tethered to a stake in the centre of a ring where it was goaded into a fury by onlookers. A Bulldog, similar in appearance to today's only larger, would then be set to it. The idea was for the dog to clamp it's jaws on the bull's nose or mouth and for the bull to exhaust itself in it's efforts to shake it off. The Bulldog had been specially bred to have jaws that locked when they were engaged and, so, once the dog had taken firm hold he would be flung into the air but his grip could rarely be broken.

This appalling sport was banned in the early nineteenth century but this did result in a decline in the Bulldog's numbers. However, it was soon realised that this breed had more to offer than it's prowess in the bull ring and conscientious breeding began.

The Bulldog of today harbours no trace of his gruesome beginnings and is perfectly trustworthy with all age groups. Exercise should be very regular but not too frantic as heart attacks can sometimes result. He is a dog of great character and prescence who enjoys human company and he makes an easy going, faithful companion.

KEY TO CHARACTER	
INTELLIGENCE	****
TEMPERAMENT	*****
EASE OF COAT CARE	*****
SUITABILITY FOR SMALL DWELLING	****
***** (5) = VERY GOOD	

BRITISH KENNEL CLUB STANDARD

BULLDOG

GENERAL APPEARANCE. — In forming a judgment on any specimen of the breed, the general appearance, which is the first impression the dog makes as a whole on the eye of the judge, should be first considered. Secondly should be noticed its size, shape and make, or rather its proportions in the relation they bear to each other. No point should be so much in excess of the others as to destroy the general symmetry, or make the dog appear deformed, or interfere with its powers of motion, etc. Thirdly its style, carriage, gait, temper and its several points should be considered separately in detail, due allowance being made for the bitch, which is not so grand or as well developed as the dog.

Thegeneral appearance of the Bulldog is that of a smooth-coated, thick-set dog, rather low in stature, but broad, powerful, and compact. The head strikingly massive and large in proportion to the dog's size.. The face extremely short. The muzzle very broad, blunt, and inclined upwards. The body short and well knit; the limbs stout and muscular. The hindquarters high and strong but rather lightly made in comparison with its heavily made foreparts. The dog should convey an impression of determination, strength, and activity, similar to that suggested by the appearance of a thick-set Ayreshire Bull.

From its formation the dog has a peculiar heavy and constrained gait, appearing to walk with short, quick steps on the tips of its toes, its hind-feet not being lifted high, but appearing to skim the ground, and running with the right shoulder rather advanced, similar to the manner of a horse in cantering.

Head and Skull. — The skull should be very large — the larger the better — and in circumference should measure (round in front of the ears) at least the height of the dog at the shoulders. Viewed from the front it should appear very high from the corner of the lower jaw to the apex of the skull, and also very broad and square. The cheeks should be well rounded and extended sideways beyond the eyes. Viewed at the side, the head should appear very high, and very short from its back to the point of the nose. The forehead should be flat, neither prominent nor overhanging the face; the skin upon it and about the head very loose and well wrinkled. The projections of the frontal bones should be very prominent, broad, square, and high, causing a deep and wide indentation between the eyes termed the "stop". From the "stop" a furrow both broad and deep should extend up to the middle of the skull, being traceable to the apex. The face, measured from the front of the cheek-bone to the nose, should be as short as possible, and its skin should be deeply and closely wrinkled. The muzzle should be short, broad, turned upwards and very deep from the corner of the eye to the corner of the mouth. The nose should be large, broad and black, and under no circumstances should it be liver coloured or brown; its top should be deeply set back almost between the eyes. The distance from the inner corner of the eye (or from the centre of the stop between the eyes) to the extreme tip of the nose should not exceed the length from the tip of the nose to the edge of the under lip. The nostrils should be large, wide, and black, with a well-defined vertical straight line between them. The flews, called the "chop" should be thick, broad, pendant, and very deep, hanging completely over the lower jaw at the sides (not in front). They should join the under lip in front and quite cover the teeth. The jaws should be broad, massive and square, the lower jaw should project considerably in front of the upper and turn up. Viewed from the front, the various properties of the face must be equally balanced on either side of an imaginary line down the centre of the face.

Eyes. — The eyes seen from the front, should be situated low down in the skull, as far from the ears as possible. The eyes and "stop" should be in the same straight line, which should be at right angles to the furrow. They should be as wide apart as possible, provided their outer corners are within the ouline of the cheeks. They should be quite round in shape, of moderate size, neither sunken nor prominent, and in colour should be very dark — almost, if not quite, black, showing no white when looking directly forward.

Ears. — The ears should be set high on the head — i.e., the front inner edge of each ear should (as viewed from the front) join the outline of the skull at the top corner of such outline, so as to place them as wide apart, and as high and as far from the eyes as possible. In size they should be small and thin. The shape termed "rose ear" is correct, and folds inwards at its back, the upper or front edge curving over outwards and backwards, showing part of the inside of the burr.

Mouth. — The jaw should be broad and square and have the six small front teeth between the canines in an even row. The canine teeth or tusks wide apart. The teeth should not be seen when the mouth is closed. The teeth should be large and strong. When viewed from the front, the underjaw should be centrally under the upper jaw to which it should also be parallel.

Neck. — Should be moderate in length (rather short than long) very thick, deep and strong. It should be well arched at the back, with much loose, thick and wrinkled skin about the throat, forming a dewlap on each side, from the lower jaw to the chest.

Forequarters. — The shoulders should be broad, sloping and deep, very powerful and muscular, and giving the appearance of having been "tacked on" to the body. The brisket should be capacious, round and very deep from the top of the shoulders to the lowest part where it joins the chest, and be well let down between forelegs. It should be large in diameter and round behind the forelegs (not flat-sided, the ribs being well rounded). The forelegs should be very stout and strong, set wide apart, thick, muscular, and straight, with well-developed forearms, presenting a rather bowed outline, but the bones of the legs should be large and straight, not bandy or curved. They should b rather short in proportion to the hind-legs, but not so short as to make the back appear long, or detract from the dog's activity, and so cripple him. The elbows should be low, and stand well away from the ribs. The pasterns should be short, straight and strong.

Body. — The chest should be very wide, laterally round, prominent, and deep, making the dog appear very broad and short-legged in front. The body should be well ribbed up behind, with the belly tucked up and not pendulous. The back should be short and strong, very broad at the shoulders, and comparatively narrow at the loins. There should be a slight fall to the back close behind the shoulders (its lowest part), whence the spine should rise to the loins (the top of which should be higher than the top of the shoulders), thence curving again more suddenly to the tail, forming an arch — a distinctive characteristic of the breed — termed "roach back".

Hindquarters. — the legs should be large and muscular, and longer in proportion than the forelegs, so as to elevate the loins. The hocks should be slightly bent and well let down, so as to be long and muscular from the loins to the point of the hock. The lower part of the leg should be short, straight and strong. The stifles should be round and turned slightly outwards away from the body. The hocks are thereby made to approach each other, and the hind feet to turn outwards.

Feet. — The hind feet, like the fore feet, should be round and compact, with the toes well split up and the knuckles prominent. The fore feet should be straight and turn very slightly outward, of medium size and moderately round. The toes compact and thick, being well split up, making the knuckles prominent and high.

Tail. — The tail, termed the "stern", should be set on low, jut out rather straight, then turn downwards. It should be round, smooth and devoid of fringe or coarse hair. It should be moderate in length — rather short than long — thick at the root, and tapering quickly to a fine point. It should have a downward carriage (not having a decided upward curve at the end), and the dog should not be able to raise it over its back.

Coat. — Should be fine in texture, short, close and smooth (hard only from the shortness and closeness, not wiry).

Colour. — The colour should be whole or smut (that is, a whole colour with a black mask or muzzle). The only colours (which should be brilliant and pure of their sort) are whole colours — viz., brindles, reds, with their varieties, fawns, fallows, etc., white and also pied (i.e., a combination of white with any other of the foregoing colours). Dudley, black and black with tan are extremely undesirable colours.

Weight and Size. — The most desirable weight for the Bulldog is 25 kg (55 lbs) for a dog and 22.7 kg (50 lbs) for a bitch.

Note. — Male animals should have two apparently normal testicles fully descended into the scrotum.

MAIN AMERICAN KENNEL CLUB VARIATION TO STANDARD FOR THE BULLDOG —

Size. — The size for mature dogs is about 50 pounds for mature bitches about 40 pounds.

BULLDOG REGISTRATIONS 1981 — 87 INCLUSIVE

1981 — 805
1982 — 832
1983 — 792
1984 — 888
1985 — 1003
1986 — 1003
1987 — 1040

CRUFTS BEST-IN-SHOW WINNER

1952 CH. NOWAYS CHUCKLES — J.T. BARNARD

CHOW CHOW

It is very possible that this breed goes back to the eleventh century B.C. that being when the first mention of Chow Chow type dogs was made. Due to the area of origin being in the remote areas of northern China, hard facts on his history are hard come by. But he was used probably in hunting and as a guard dog with an almost certain link with the dogs of the Arctic, his coat and great physical strength giving weight to this theory. There are some rare blue Chow Chows in China, but these are not to be seen in Britain. He was first recognised in this country in 1894 and from then until the second World War he was extremely popular. He is still very much in evidence but not quite to the same extent.

The straight hind leg formation of the Chow Chow gives him a distinctive rather wooden gait, but this somehow adds to his imposing physique and earnest expression. The indigo blue tongue of this breed is unique to him.

The Chow Chow is a breed of rugged beauty and will respond to strong-minded thoughtful training. However, he is not to be recommended to families with small children as he can be a little impatient with them and a Chow Chow's bite is not be be flirted with.

Abhorrent as it is to contemplate, this excellent breed has been used as a food source in it's native China.

KEY TO CHARACTER

INTELLIGENCE	***
TEMPERAMENT	***
EASE OF COAT CARE	*
SUITABILITY FOR SMALL DWELLING	**

***** (5) = VERY GOOD

BRITISH KENNEL CLUB STANDARD

CHOW CHOW

CHARACTERISTICS. — A well-balanced dog, leonine in appearance, with proud dignified bearing; loyal yet aloof; unique in its stilted gait and bluish-black tongue.

GENERAL APPEARANCE. — An active, compact, short-coupled and well-balanced dog, well knit in frame, with tail carried well over the back.

Head and Skull. — Skull flat and broad, with little stop, well filled out under the eyes. Muzzle moderate in length, broad from the eyes to the point (not pointed at the end like a fox). Nose black, large and wide in all cases (with the exception of cream and white in which case a light-coloured nose is permissible and in blues and fawns a self-coloured nose); but in all colours a black nose is preferable.

Eyes. — Dark and small, preferably almond-shaped (in blue or fawn dog a light colour is permissible).

Ears. — Small, thick, slightly rounded at the tip, carried stiffly erect but placed well forward over the eyes and wide apart, which gives the dog the peculiar characteristic expression of the breed, viz., a scowl.

Mouth. — Teeth strong and level, giving scissor bite. Tongue bluish black. Flews and roof of mouth black. Gums preferably black.

Neck. — Strong, full, set well on the shoulders and slightly arched.

Forequarters. — Shoulders muscular and sloping. Forelegs perfectly straight of moderate length and with good bone.

Body. — Chest broad and deep. Back short, straight and strong. Loins powerful.

Bulldog
Chow Chow

Dalmatian
French Bulldog

Hindquarters. — Hindlegs muscular and hocks well let down and perfectly straight which are essential in order to produce the Chow's characteristic stilted gait.

Feet. — Small, round and catlike, standing well on the toes.

Tail. — Set high and carried well over the back.

Coat. — Abundant, dense, straight and stand-off. Outer coat rather coarse in texture and with a soft woolly undercoat. The Chow Chow is a profusely coated dog and balance should therefore be assessed when the coat is at its natural length.

Colour. — Whole coloured black, red, blue, fawn, cream or white, frequently shaded but not in patches or parti-coloured (the underpart of tail and back of thighs frequently of a light colour).

Weight and Size. — Minimum height for Chows to be 45.7 cm (18″) but in every case balance should be the outstanding feature and height left to the discretion of the judges.

Faults. — Drop ears, tongue splashed or patchy, tail not carried over the back, parti-coloured, off black noses except in the colours specified, viz., creams, whites, blues or fawns. Any artificial shortening of the coat which alters the natural outline or expression of the dog should be penalised. (The standard of the smooth variety is identical with the above except that the coat is smooth).

Note. — Male animals should have two apparently normal testicles fully descended into the scrotum.

CHOW CHOW REGISTRATIONS 1981 — 87 INCLUSIVE

1981 — 1155
1982 — 1096
1983 — 1096
1984 — 929
1985 — 977
1986 — 942
1987 — 773

CRUFTS BEST-IN-SHOW

1936 CH. CHOONAM HUNG KWONG — MRS. V.A.M. MANOOCH

DALMATIAN

The Dalmatian is an energetic, loyal and affectionate breed, with a genuine liking for people of all ages.

His history is uncertain, with serveral differing views being voiced. Despite his name, it is now thought unlikely that he comes from the Yugoslavian province of Dalmatia, the British having probably introduced him there. Some contend that he has Danish origins, others favour the eastern Mediterranean regions. It is possible that the Dalmatian has existed in a fairly unaltered form for many hundreds of years. A spotted dog can be seen in many paintings dating from the 17th century and before and some of these were quite similar to today's specimens.

In the 19th century the Dalmatian was widely known as the "carriage dog". This nickname stems from his apparent affinity for horses, and a liking for running alongside them as they pulled the coaches of the gentry. It became extremely fashionable, in fact, to be seen with Dalmatians accompanying you in this way.

All Dalmatian owners will testify to the breed's affable, playful disposition and equally to it's surprisingly forceful guarding qualities. They are lively, highly strung dogs with endless stamina, so exercise is of a paramount importance. With application they can be trained into excellent house dogs, especially enjoying the company of children, who cope well with their endless appetite for play.

KEY TO CHARACTER	
INTELLIGENCE	***
TEMPERAMENT	***
EASE OF COAT CARE	*****
SUITABILITY FOR SMALL DWELLING	**
***** (5) = VERY GOOD	

BRITISH KENNEL CLUB STANDARD

DALMATIAN

GENERAL APPEARANCE. — The Dalmatian should be a balanced, strong, muscular, active dog of good demeanour. Symmetrical in outline, free from coarseness and lumber, capable of great endurance with a fair amount of speed.

Head and Skull. — The head should be of fair length, the skull flat, reasonably broad between the ears but refined, moderately well defined at the temples, i.e. exhibiting a moderate amount of Stop; not in one straight line from nose to occiput bone. Entirely free from wrinkle. The muzzle should be long and powerful, never snipy, the lips clean, fitting the jaw moderately close. The nose in the black-spotted variety should always be black, in the liver spotted variety always brown.

Eyes. — The eyes, set moderately well apart should be of medium size, round, bright and sparkling, with an intelligent expression, their colour, depending on the marking of the dog; dark in the black spotted, amber in the liver spotted. The rim round the eyes should be complete; black in the black spotted and liver brown in the liver spotted.

Ears. — The ears should be set on rather high, of moderate size, rather wide at the base, gradually tapering to a rounded point. Fine in texture, carried close to the head. The marking should be well broken up, preferably spotted.

Mouth. — The teeth should meet. The upper slightly overlapping the lower (Scissor bite).

Neck. — The neck should be fairly long, nicely arched, light and tapering. Entirely free from throatiness.

Forequarters. — The shoulders should be moderately oblique, clean and muscular. Elbows close to the body. The forelegs perfectly straight with strong round bone down to the feet, with a slight spring at the pastern joint.

Body. — The chest should not be too wide but deep and capacious with plenty of lung and heart room. The ribs well sprung, well defined wither, powerful level back, loins strong, clean and muscular, and slightly arched.

Hindquarters. — Rounded, muscles clean with well developed second thigh, good turn of stifle and hocks well defined.

Tail. — In length reaching approximately to the hocks. Stong at the insertion gradually tapering towards the end, it should not be inserted too low or too high, be free from coarseness and carried with a slight upward curve, never curled. Preferably spotted.

Feet. — Round, compact, with well arched toes (cat feet) and round tough elastic pads. Nails black or white in the black spotted variety, in the liver spotted variety — brown or white.

Gait. — The Dalmatian should have great freedom of movement. A smooth, powerful rhythmic action with a long stride. Viewed from behind, the legs should move in parallel the hindlegs tracking the fore. A short stride and paddling action is incorrect.

Coat. — The coat should be short, hard and dense, sleek and glossy in appearance. The ground colour should be pure white. Black spotted dogs should have dense black spots and liver spotted dogs liver-brown spots. They should not run together but be round and well defined the size of sixpence to a half crown, as well distributed as possible. Spots on the extremities should be smaller than those on the body.

Size. — Overall balance of prime importance, but the ideal height to be aimed at is: Dog 58.4 cm to 61 cm (23″ to 24″). Bitch 55.9 cm to 58.4 cm (22″ to 23″).

Faults. — Patches, black and liver spots on the same dog (tri colours). Lemon spots; Blue eyes; Bronzing and other faults of pigmentation.

Note. — Male animals should have two apparently normal testicles fully descended into the scrotum.

SCALE OF POINTS

Build and symmetry 20
Colour 20
Head and expression 9
Spotted ears 4
Neck and breast 10
Legs and feet 15
Forequarters 8
Hindquarters 8
Spotted tail 6

Total   100

MAIN AMERICAN KENNEL CLUB VARIATION TO STANDARD FOR THE DALMATIAN —

Size. — The desirable height of dogs and bitches is between 19 and 23 inches at the withers.

DALMATIAN REGISTRATIONS 1981 — 87 INCLUSIVE

1981 — 745
1982 — 699
1983 — 756
1984 — 681
1985 — 911
1986 — 752
1987 — 773

CRUFTS BEST IN SHOW WINNER

1968 CH. FANHILL FAUNE — MRS. E.J. WOODYATT

FRENCH BULLDOG

Although he carries the name of French Bulldog, this breed is a direct descendant of the early British Bulldog. It is believed that over three hundred years ago small Bulldog specimens were imported by the French and crossed with dogs native to France. Exactly which crossings took place is unclear although the accent was always on keeping the size down. As was the unhappy fate of many bull breeds, the French Bulldog was often used for pit fighting. This was not surprising as he possesses all the courage and pound-for-pound strength of his larger cousins.

It was not until the early 1900's that the breed was registered with the Kennel Club in Britain and it was only a short time before then that the first French Bulldogs appeared in the U.S.A. The breed has built up a solid following in both countries.

Apart from the very conspicuous and appealing bat-ears, the French Bulldog is almost a Bulldog in miniature both in his physical proportions and in his friendly, outgoing nature. He makes a lively companion who loves rough and tumble games and the company of children. He is a good choice of pet for someone who wants a small dog that has no trace of frailty or timidity. If his owner's family indulge in his play sessions, then the French Bulldog will derive a good deal of exercise from this, but he will still enjoy plenty of outdoor excursions.

KEY TO CHARACTER	
INTELLIGENCE	****
TEMPERAMENT	*****
EASE OF COAT CARE	*****
SUITABILITY FOR SMALL DWELLING	*****
***** (5) = VERY GOOD	

BRITISH KENNEL CLUB STANDARD

FRENCH BULLDOG

GENERAL APPEARANCE. — A French Bulldog should be sound, active and intelligent, of compact build, medium or small sized, with good bone, a short smooth coat, and the various points so evenly balanced that the dog does not look ill-proportioned.

Head and Skull. — Head massive, square and broad. Skull nearly flat between the ears, with a domed forehead, the loose skin forming symmetrical wrinkles. Muzzle broad, deep and laid back with the muscles of the cheek well developed; nose and lips black. Stop well defined. Lower jaw should be deep square, broad, slightly undershot and well turned up. Nose extremely short, black and wide, with open nostrils and the line between well defined. Lips thick, the lower meeting the upper in the middle, completely hiding the teeth. The upper lip should cover the lower on each side with plenty of cushion, but not so exaggerated as to hang too much below the level of the lower jaw.

Eyes. — Should be dark, of moderate size, round, neither sunken nor prominent showing no white when looking straight, set wide apart and low down in the skull.

Ears. — "Bat ears" of medium size, wide at the base, rounded at the top, set high, carried upright and parallel, a sufficient width of skull preventing them being too close together; the skin soft and fine and the orifice, as seen from the front, showing entirely.

Mouth. — Teeth sound and regular, but not visible when the mouth is closed. Tongue must not protrude.

Neck. — Should be powerful, with loose skin at the throat, but not exaggerated. Well arched and thick, but not too short.

Forequarters. — Legs set wide apart, straight boned, strong, muscular and short.

Body. — Should be short, cobby, muscular and well rounded, with deep wide brisket, roach back, strong, wide at the shoulders and narrowing at the loins, good "cut up" and well sprung.

Hindquarters. — Legs strong, muscular and longer than the forelegs so as to raise the loins above th shoulders. Hocks well let down and with very fine movement.

Feet. — Should be small, compact and placed in continuation of the line of the leg, with absolutely sound pasterns. The hind rather longer than the fore-feet. Toes compact, knuckle high, nails short, thick and preferably black.

Tail. — Very short, set low, thick at the root, and tapering quickly towards the tip, either straight or kinked, but never curling over the back. A good tail is placed so that it cannot be carried gaily.

Coat. — Texture fine, smooth, lustrous, short and close.

Colour. — The colours allowed are brindle, pied and fawn.

(1) The brindle is a mixture of black and coloured hairs. This variety may contain white on condition that brindle predominates.

(2) The pied is a dog in which the white predominates over the brindle. White dogs are classified with the pieds, but their eyelashes and eyerims should be black. In pieds the white should be clear with definite brindle patches and no ticking or black spots.

(3) The fawn dog may contain brindle hairs but must have black eyerims and eyelashes.

Weight and Size. — The ideal weight is 12.7 kg (28 lbs) for dogs and 10.9 kg (24 lbs) for bitches but soundness must not be sacrificed to smallness.

Faults. — Nose other than black. Eyes of different colours. Ears not erect. Hare lip. Tail docked. Colour-Tan, Mouse Grey (blue).

Note. — Male animals should have two apparently normal testicles fully descended into the scrotum.

MAIN AMERICAN KENNEL CLUB VARIATION TO STANDARD FOR THE FRENCH BULLDOG —

Weight. — A lightweight class under 22 pounds; heavyweight class, 22 pounds, and not over 28 pounds.

FRENCH BULLDOG REGISTRATIONS — 1981 — 87 INCLUSIVE

1981 — 14i
1982 — 128
1983 — 103
1984 — 146
1985 — 123
1986 — 163
1987 — 176

YET TO WIN CRUFTS BEST-IN-SHOW.

JAPANESE SPITZ

At first glance, the Japanese Spitz looks very much like a Samoyed in miniature. This is not surprising since both dogs belong to the Spitz group and therefore share the same ancestry. This ancestry lies in the dogs of the Arctic regions and it seems probable that dogs reached Japan centuries ago from northern Europe to be later developed into something close to today's Japanese Spitz.

Outside Japan, this breed is very uncommon, although in Britain he is beginning to make headway in the show world. He is very suited to the show-ring with his luxurious white coat and his air of alertness and intelligence.

As with all the Spitz breeds, he is not short on courage and energy and in the home he makes an engaging pet. He does not tolerate strangers easily and becomes very strongly attached to his owner. He enjoys the outdoor life but can live in the town if allowed plenty of outings.

Despite the length of the coat, grooming is not too much of a headache but a frequent brushing is necessary to keep the Japanese Spitz at his impressive best.

KEY TO CHARACTER	
INTELLIGENCE	****
TEMPERAMENT	****
EASE OF COAT CARE	***
SUITABILITY FOR SMALL DWELLING	***
***** (5) = VERY GOOD	

BRITISH KENNEL CLUB STANDARD

JAPANESE SPITZ

CHARACTERISTICS. — Intelligent, bold, and lively.

GENERAL APPEARANCE. — Profuse, pure white offstanding coat. The dog should have a sharply pointed muzzle and triangular shaped ears standing erect. Bushy tail carried over the back. The overall quality of the body should be firm and strong, full of flexibility. Fore and hind quarters should be well proportioned and balanced.

Head and Skull. — Head of medium size without coarseness; moderately broad and slightly rounded. Skull broadest at occiput; well defined stop; cheeks rounded; forehead not protruding. Muzzle sharply pointed neither too thick nor too long. Lips firm and tightly closed, with black colour desirable. The nose round and small and black in pigmentation.

Eyes. — Of moderate size, almond shape, set rather obliquely and not too wide apart; dark in colour with black eye rims.

Ears. — Small, triangular and standing erect. Set high, forward facing and not too wide apart.

Mouth. — The jaws should be strong, with a perfect regular and complete scissor bite, i.e. the upper teeth closely overlapping the lower teeth and set square to the jaw.

Neck. — Strong and of moderate length.

Forequarters. — Shoulders well laid. Forelegs straight with elbows firm and tight and pasterns slightly sloping.

Body. — Chest broad and deep. Ribs powerfully sprung; belly moderately firm with good tuck-up. Withers should be highly developed and back should be straight and short. Loins should be broad and firm. Croup should be comparatively long and slightly arched.

Hindquarters. — Muscular and moderately angulated. Hind legs paralled to each other viewed from the rear.

Feet. — Toes should be small, round and cat-like. Well padded with good pigment. Nails should be hard and black or dark.

Gait. — Light and nimble, active, energetic and very smooth.

Tail. — Moderate in length with root set high and curled over the back.

Coat. — The outer coat should be straight and stand-off. Profuse undercoat, short, dense and soft in texture. Shorter on the face, ears, front parts of fore and hind legs and below hocks. All the other parts of the body covered with long coat. Mane on the neck and shoulder, reaching down to the brisket. Tail profusely covered with long hair.

Colour. — Pure white.

Size. — Height at shoulder: 30 to 40 cm (12″ to 16″) for males, 25 to 35 cm (10″ to 14″) for females.

Faults. — Any departure from the foregoing points should be considered a fault and the seriousness with which the fault is regarded should be in exact proportion to its degree.

Note. — Male animals should have two apparently normal testicles fully descended into the scrotum.

JAPANESE SPITZ REGISTRATIONS 1981 — 87 INCLUSIVE

1981 — 41
1982 — 77
1983 — 106
1984 — 109
1985 — 219
1986 — 143
1987 — 180

YET TO WIN CRUFTS BEST-IN-SHOW.

KEESHOND

This member of the Spitz family of breeds hails from Holland. During his early history the Keeshond was used extensively as a guard dog on the barges of Holland's many canals. His alertness and loud bark were well suited to this post and his medium size was sufficient to back up his agression.

The breed's name is taken from a famous dog lover called Kees de Gyselaer who was a leading dutch patriot in the 18th century when Holland was on the verge of upheaval.

The wild arctic ancestry of the Keeshond has long since vanished from his character and centuries of working for man and living with his families have produced a first class house dog. His temperament is usually very sound and house training and indeed training for the show bench, is no problem. He becomes very attached to his owner, often being a little wary of strangers but he will live harmoniously with all the owner's family.

The glorious, dense double coat is obviously an asset in the winter and when given fairly regular attention is the Keeshond's most striking feature.

Feeding and exercise requirements are not excessive and he could be said to be generally an easily managed breed.

KEY TO CHARACTER	
INTELLIGENCE	***
TEMPERAMENT	*****
EASE OF COAT CARE	**
SUITABILITY FOR SMALL DWELLING	***
***** (5) = VERY GOOD	

BRITISH KENNEL CLUB STANDARD

KEESHOND

GENERAL APPEARANCE. — A short, compact body; alert carriage, foxlike head; small pointed ears; a well-feathered, curling tail, carried over the back; hair very thick on the neck, forming a large ruff; head, ears and lets covered with short thick hair. Dogs should move cleanly and briskly (not lope like an Alsatian) but movement should be straight and sharp. Dogs should show boldly.

Head and Skull. — Head well proportioned to the body, wedge-shaped when seen from above; from the side showing definite stop. Muzzle should be of medium length, neither coarse nor snipy.

Eyes. — Dark with well-defined spectacles.

Ears. — Small and well set on head, not wide and yet not meeting.

Mouth. — Should be neither over nor undershot, upper teeth should just overlap under teeth and should be white, sound and strong (but discoloration from distemper not to penalize severely).

Forequarters. — Forelegs feathered, straight, with good bone and cream in colour.

Hindquarters. — Hind legs should be straight, showing very little hock and not feathered below the hock. Cream in colour.

Feet. — Round and cat-like with black nails.

Tail. — Tightly curled, a double curl at the end is desirable. Plume to be white on the top where curled, with black tip.

Coat. — Dense, and harsh (off-standing), dense ruff and well feathered, profuse trousers; a soft, thick, light-coloured undercoat. Coat should not be silky, wavy or woolly, nor should it form a parting on the back.

Colour. — Should be wolf, ash-grey; not all black or all white, and markings should be definite.

Weight and Size. — The ideal height is 45.7 cm (18″) for dogs and 43.2 cm (17″) for bitches, but type is of more importance.

Faults. — Light eyes, prominent eyes. Curly or wavy tendency in coat. Silky coat. Absence of spectacles. Nervous demeanour. Drop ears. Whole white foot or feet. Black marks below the knee, pencilling excepted. White chest. Apple head or absence of stop.

Note. — Male animals should have two apparently normal testicles fully descended into the scrotum.

KEESHOND REGISTRATIONS 1981 — 87 INCLUSIVE

1981 — 198
1982 — 142
1983 — 216
1984 — 253
1985 — 177
1986 — 242
1987 — 221

CRUFTS BEST-IN-SHOW WINNER

1957 CH. VOLKRIJK OF VORDEN — MRS. I.M. TUCKER.

LHASA APSO

This is another of the attractive small dogs that has his roots in Tibet. The Lhasa Apso was the favourite breed of the Dalai Lama, the supreme religious leader of Tibet. There are many stories of some of the finest Lhasa Apso specimens being presented as gifts to visiting Europeans and this is most probably how this breed reached the west. After the Chinese takeover of Tibet and the exile of the Dalai Lama, it has not been clear how these dogs are faring, but certainly before the invasion they were held in the highest regard by the monks who kept them in their monastries.

Nowadays in Britain, the Lhasa Apso has become quite well established and has been a great success in the show world. The solid little frame is covered with an abundant coat which is hard in texture yet flows beautifully smooth and straight when correctly groomed. It is mainly this feature which has always guaranteed these dogs a second look by all who attend breed shows.

The Lhasa Apso is a dog with a self confidence which belies his stature and he is often aloof with strangers. His loyalty to his owner is very pronounced and he will adopt a guarding role whenever necessary. Within the family he mixes well with all age groups and he will enjoy lengthy sessions of play in the home. This play should be supplemented with frequent walks. To do the Lhasa Apso full justice, the coat must be given a great deal of attention.

KEY TO CHARACTER	
INTELLIGENCE	***
TEMPERAMENT	****
EASE OF COAT CARE	*
SUITABILITY FOR SMALL DWELLING	*****
***** (5) = VERY GOOD	

BRITISH KENNEL CLUB STANDARD
LHASA APSO

CHARACTERISTICS. — The Apso should give the appearance of a well-balanced, solid dog. Gay and assertive, but chary of strangers. Free and jaunty in movement.

Head and Skull. — Heavy head furnishings with good fall over the eyes, good whiskers and beard.

Skull moderately narrow, falling away behind the eyes in a marked degree; not quite flat, but not domed or apple shaped.

Straight foreface, with medium stop. Nose black. Muzzle about 1½ inches long, but not square; the length from tip of nose to be roughly one-third the total length from nose to back of skull.

Eyes. — Dark. Medium sized eyes to be frontally placed, not large or full, or small and sunk. No white showing at base or top of eye.

Ears. — Pendant, heavily feathered. Dark tips an asset.

Mouth. — Upper incisors should close just inside the lower, i.e., a reverse scissor bite. Incisors should be nearly in a staight line. Full dentition is desirable.

Neck. — Strong, well covered with a dense mane which is more pronounced in dogs than in bitches.

Forequarters. — Shoulders should be well laid back. Forelegs straight, heavily furnished with hair.

Body. — The length from point of shoulders to point of buttocks greater than height at withers. Well ribbed up. Level top-line. Strong loin. Well balanced and compact.

Hindquarters. — Well developed with good muscle. Good angulation. Heavily furnished. The hocks when viewed from behind should be parallel and not too close together.

Feet. — Round and cat-like, with good pads. Well-feathered.

Tail. — High set, carried well over back and not like a pot-hook. There is often a kink at the end. Well feathered.

Coat. — Top coat heavy, straight and hard, not wooly or silky, of good length. Dense under-coat.

Colours. — Golden, sandy, honey, dark grizzle, slate, smoke, parti-colour, black, white or brown.

Size. — Ideal height: 25.4 cm (10″) at shoulder for dogs; bitches slightly smaller.

Note. — Male animals should have two apparently normal testicles fully descended into the scrotum.

MAIN AMERICAN KENNEL CLUB VARIATION TO STANDARD FOR THE LHASA APSO —

Size. — Variable, but about 10 inches or 11 inches at shoulder for dogs, bitches slightly smaller.

LHASA APSO REGISTRATIONS 1981 — 87 INCLUSIVE

1981 — 965
1982 — 952
1983 — 1303
1984 — 1304
1985 — 1404
1986 — 1485
1987 — 1447

CRUFTS BEST-IN-SHOW WINNER

1984 CH. SAXONSPRINGS HACKENSACK — MRS. J. BLYTH

MINIATURE SCHNAUZER

This attractive small breed is a scaled-down carbon copy of his larger relative the Schnauzer, sometimes called the Standard Schnauzer. It seems that to produce the Miniature Schnauzer, small Schnauzer specimens were crossed by German breeders with other small breeds. Some maintain that one of the breeds involved in this miniaturisation process was the Affenpinscher, although the Miniature Schnauzer's physical appearance might belie this.

He has the strength of character and cool temperament of a larger dog and this has ensured a very strong following for him, particularly in the U.S.A. where he is classed as a Terrier, an idea strongly resisted by European fanciers. But he does share one of the talents of the Terrier family, that of being an excellent ratter.

As a show competitor he has made a great impact. If expertly prepared the Miniature Schnauzer is a picture of smartness and he is renowned for his ability to stand statue-like for long periods. He has also shown his worth in the obedience ring.

It would be difficult to find a better small dog for a family. Apart from his grooming needs, he is easily maintained, robust and healthy. He loves playful exercise but is quite happy to have short regular walks if, for instance, his owner is elderly.

Japanese Spitz
Keeshond

Lhasa Apso
Miniature Schnauzer

KEY TO CHARACTER	
INTELLIGENCE	****
TEMPERAMENT	*****
EASE OF COAT CARE	**
SUITABILITY FOR SMALL DWELLING	*****
***** (5) = VERY GOOD	

BRITISH KENNEL CLUB STANDARD

MINIATURE SCHNAUZER

GENERAL APPEARANCE. — The Miniature Schnauzer is a powerfully built, robust, sinewy, nearly square, dog (length of body equal to height at shoulders). His temperament combines high spirits, reliability, strength, endurance and vigour. Expression keen and attitude alert. Correct conformation is of more importance than colour or other purely "beauty" points.

Head and Skull. — Head strong and elongated, gradually narrowing from the ears to the eyes and thence forward toward the tip of the nose. Upper part of the head (occiput to the base of the forehead) moderately broad between the ears — with flat, creaseless, forehead and well muscled, but not too strongly developed cheeks. Medium stop to accentuate prominent eyebrows. The powerful muzzle formed by the upper and lower jaws (base of forehead to the tip of the nose) should end in a moderately blunt line, with bristly, stubby moustache and chin whiskers. Ridge of the nose straight and running almost parallel to the extension of the forehead. The nose is black and full. Lips tight and not overlapping.

Eyes. — Medium sized, dark, oval, set forward, with arched bushy eyebrows.

Ears. — Neat and V shaped, set high and dropping forward to temple.

Mouth. — Scissor teeth, slightly overlapping from the top; with strongly developed fangs; healthy and pure white.

Neck. — Moderately long, nape strong and slightly arched, skin close to throat, neck set cleanly on shoulders.

Forequarters. — Shoulders flat and sloping. Forelegs straight viewed from any position. Muscles smooth and lithe rather than prominent; bone strong, straight and carried well down to the feet; elbows set close to the body and pointing directly backward.

Body. — Chest moderately broad, deep, with visible strong breast bone reaching down to at least the height of elbow and slightly rising backward to loins. Back strong and straight, slightly higher at the shoulder than at the hindquarters, with short, well developed loins. Ribs well sprung. Length of body equal to height from top of withers to ground.

Hindquarters. — Thighs slanting and flat, but strongly muscled. Hindlegs (upper and lower thighs) at first vertical to the stifle, from stifle to hock, in line with the extension of the upper neck line, from hock, vertical to ground.

Feet. — Short, round, extremely compact with close-arched toes, (cat's paws), dark nails and hard soles. The feet also deep or thickly padded, pointing forward.

Tail. — Set on and carried high, cut down to three joints.

Coat. — Hard and wiry and just short enough for smartness, clean on neck, shoulder, ears and skull, plenty of good hard hair on front legs. Good undercoat is essential.

Colour. — All pepper and salt colours in even proportions, or pure black.

Height. — The ideal height for bitches shall be 33 cm (13") and for dogs 35.6 cm (14"). Too small, toyish-appearing dogs are not typical and should be penalised.

Faults. — Too heavy or too light; too low or high on the leg. Head too heavy or round, creased forehead, sticking-out, or badly carried, ears; light eye, with yellow or light grey rings; strongly protruding cheek-bones; flabby throat skin; undershot or overshot jaw. Muzzle too pointed or too small. Back too long, sunken or roached; barrel-shaped ribs; slanting crupper; elbows turned out); heels turned in, hindpart overbuilt (too steep). Toes spread open; paws long and flat (hare). Coat too short and sleek, or too long, soft or curled. All white, spotty, tigered or red colours. Small white breast spot or marking is not a fault. Among other serious faults are cow-hocks, sunken pasterns, or any weakness of joint, bones or muscular development.

Note. — Male animals should have two apparently normal testicles fully descended into the scrotum.

MAIN AMERICAN KENNEL CLUB VARIATION TO STANDARD FOR THE MINIATURE SCHNAUZER —

Ears. — When cropped the ears are identical in shape and length, with pointed tips.

Size. — From 12 to 14 inches. Ideal size 13½ inches.

MINIATURE SCHNAUZER REGISTRATIONS 1981 — 87 INCLUSIVE

1981 —	751
1982 —	813
1983 —	907
1984 —	943
1985 —	1192
1986 —	1214
1987 —	1192

YET TO WIN CRUFTS BEST-IN-SHOW.

Poodle

Schipperke

POODLE

The official standard for all three types of Poodle is exactly the same save for the obvious height differences. The first Standard Poodle was registered in 1874, the first Miniature in 1911 and the first Toy in 1957.

A similar breed seems to have reared it's head in the 16th century. This cannot be substantiated, however, as many early poodle-like dogs depicted in paintings and engravings might well have been more closely related to the Portugese water dog which is often clipped similarly to a poodle.

Both the French and the Germans stake a claim to being the Poodle's originator, and until recently it was common to hear the breed referred to as the French Poodle. But Germany has a strong case for there is record of an ancient German breed known as the Pudel, the name changing to Poedel when the breed sprang up in Belgium and Holland.

Surprising as it may seem, the Poodle has been successfully employed as a hunting dog, having excellent retrieving qualities. His intelligence is beyond question as is clearly illustrated by the amazingly complex tricks performed by circus poodles. His athleticism, too, is displayed at these shows.

If shown plenty of affection and attention, the Poodle makes a truly interesting companion, but they can become touchy if left too long to their own devices.

The coat can be clipped in a variety of different styles with perhaps the most popular being the "Lion Clip", so called as it features a heavy mane around the neck and shoulders.

The three Poodle varieties offer a good choice for many prospective owners, with the Toy being currently the most popular, due to his manageable size and undemanding exercise needs.

KEY TO CHARACTER		
INTELLIGENCE		*****
TEMPERAMENT		***
EASE OF COAT CARE		*
SUITABILITY FOR SMALL DWELLING	STANDARD	*
	MINIATURE	****
	TOY	*****
***** (5) = VERY GOOD		

BRITISH KENNEL CLUB STANDARD

POODLE (STANDARD)

CHARACTERISTICS & GENERAL APPEARANCE. — That of a very active, intelligent, well balanced and elegant looking dog with good temperament, carrying himself very proudly.

Gait. — Sound, free movement and light gait are essential.

Head and Skull. — Long and fine with slight peak at the back. The skull not broad and with a moderate stop. Foreface strong and well chiselled, not falling away under the eyes; bones and muscle flat. Lips tight fitting. Chin well defined, but not protruding. The whole head must be in proportion to the size of the dog.

Eyes. — Almond shaped, dark, not set too close together, full of fire and intelligence.

Ears. — The leather long and wide, low set on, hanging close to the face.

Mouth. — Teeth — white, strong, even, with scissor bite. A full set of 42 teeth is desirable.

Neck. — Well proportioned, of good length and strong to admit of the head being carried high and with dignity. Skin fitting tightly at the throat.

Forequarters. — Shoulders — strong and muscular, sloping well to the back, legs set straight from the shoulders, well muscled.

Body. — Chest — deep and moderately wide. Ribs — well sprung and rounded. Back — short, strong, slightly hollowed, loins broad and muscular.

Hindquarters. — Thighs well developed and muscular, well bent stifles, well let down hocks, hind legs turning neither in nor out.

Schnauzer

Shih Tzu

Feet. — Pasterns strong, tight feet proportionately small, oval in shape, turning neither in nor out, toes arched, pads thick and hard, well cushioned.

Tail. — Set on rather high, well carried at a slight angle away from the body, never curled or carried over the back, thick at the root.

Coat. — Very profuse and dense of good harsh texture without knots or tangles. All short hair close, thick and curly. It is strongly recommended that the traditional lion clip be adhered to.

Colour. — All solid colours. White and cream poodles to have black nose, lips and eyerims, black toenails desirable, brown poodles to have dark amber eyes, dark liver nose, lips, eyerims and toenails. Apricot poodles to have dark eyes with black points or deep amber eyes with liver points. Black, silver and blue poodles to have black nose, lips, eyerims and toenails. Cream, apricot, born, silver and blue poodles may show varying shades of the same colour up to 18 months. Clear colours preferred.

Size. — 38 cm (15") and over.

Faults. — Heavy build, clumsiness, long back, snipy in foreface, light or round or prominent eyes, lippiness, bad carriage, heavy gait, coarse head, over or undershot or pincer mouth, flesh coloured nose, coarse legs and feet, long flat toes, open soft coats with no curl, particolours — white markings on black or coloured poodles, lemon or other markings on white poodles, vicious temperament.

Note. — Male animals should have two apparently normal testicles fully descended into the scrotum.

POODLE (MINIATURE)

The Poodle (Miniature) should be in every respect a replica, in miniature, of the Poodle (Standard). Height at shoulder should be under 38 cm (15") but not under 28 cm (11").

POODLE (TOY)

The standard of the Poodle (Toy) is the same as that of the Poodle (Standard) and Poodle (Miniature) except that the height at shoulder should be under 28 cm (11").

MAIN AMERICAN KENNEL CLUB VARIATION TO STANDARD FOR THE POODLE —

Size. — The Miniature Poodle is 15 inches or under at the highest point of the shoulders, with a minimum height in excess of 10 inches. The Toy Poodle is 10 inches or under at the highest point of the shoulders.

STANDARD POODLE REGISTRATIONS 1981 — 87 INCLUSIVE

1981 —   794
1982 —   745
1983 —   923
1984 —   885
1985 — 1103
1986 — 1103
1987 — 1113

CRUFTS BEST-IN-SHOW WINNER TWICE

1955 CH. TZIGANE AGGRI OF NASHEND — MRS. A. PROCTOR
1985 CH. MONTRAVIA TOMMY-GUN — MISS M. GIBBS.

MINIATURE POODLE REGISTRATIONS 1981 — 87 INCLUSIVE

1981 — 1781
1982 — 1538
1983 — 1627
1984 — 1542
1985 — 1475
1986 — 1233
1987 — 1190

YET TO WIN CRUFTS BEST-IN-SHOW.

TOY POODLE REGISTRATIONS 1981 — 87 INCLUSIVE

1981 — 3567
1982 — 3100
1983 — 3037
1984 — 2799
1985 — 2740
1986 — 2166
1987 — 2162

CRUFTS BEST-IN-SHOW WINNER TWICE

1966 OAKINGTON PUCKSHILL AMBER SUNBLUSH — MRS. C.E. PERRY
1982 CH. GRAYCO HAZLENUT — MRS. L.A. HOWARD.

Tibetan Spaniel

Tibetan Terrier

SCHIPPERKE

The early history of this breed's development is open to argument but the Belgain's can rightly claim to have originated the modern Schipperke. He was used in Belgium as a watchdog and vermin controller on the canals. Their nimbleness and size enabled them to scurry around the barges with great ease and his very strong guarding instinct was put to good use. The name Schipperke is Flemish for "little skipper", a title well suited to this breed's jaunty demeanour.

He first appeared in Britain some 100 years ago and has a comparatively small, but devoted band of followers. It is perhaps surprising that registrations for the Schipperke are not higher as he has an endearing and interesting personality. He loves to play and children are perfectly safe in his company. He is far more robust than his diminutive size would indicate and longevity is well known as a Schipperke trait.

Feeding requirements and grooming needs are minimal and he will be happy with long or short periods of daily exercise, whichever the owner prefers. The tail is usually docked when very young although some dogs are born tail-less.

KEY TO CHARACTER	
INTELLIGENCE	***
TEMPERAMENT	****
EASE OF COAT CARE	*****
SUITABILI1 Y FOR SMALL DWELLING	*****
***** (5) = VERY GOOD	

BRITISH KENNEL CLUB STANDARD

SCHIPPERKE

GENERAL APPEARANCE. — A small cobby animal, with sharp expression, intensely lively, presenting the appearance of being always on the alert.

CHARACTERISTICS. — Intelligent, lively and alert.

Head and Skull. — Head foxy in type, skull not round, but fairly broad, flat and with little stop. The muzzle should be moderate in length, fine but not weak, should be well filled out under the eyes. Nose black and small.

Eyes. — Dark brown, small, more oval than round and not full; bright and full of expression.

Ears. — Sharp, of moderate length, not too broad at the base, tapering to a point. Carried stiffly erect and strong enough not be be bent other than lengthways.

Mouth. — Teeth strong and level.

Neck. — Strong and full, rather short set, broad on the shoulders, and slightly arched.

Forequarters. — Shoulders muscular and sloping. Legs perfectly straight, well under the body, with bone in proportion to the body.

Body. — Chest broad and deep in brisket. Back short, straight and strong. Loins powerful, well drawn up from brisket.

Hindquarters. — Fine compared to the foreparts, muscular and well-developed thighs; tailless rump well rounded. Legs strong, muscular, hocks well let down.

Feet. — Should be small, cat-like, and standing well on the toes.

Coat. — Abundant, dense and harsh, smooth on the head, ears and legs, lying close on the back and sides, but erect and thick round the neck, forming a mane and frill and with a good culotte on the back of the thighs.

Colour. — Should be black but other whole colours are permissible.

Weight and Size. — Weight about 5.4 to 7.3 kg (12 to 16 lbs).

Faults. — Drop or semi-erect ears, Dudley noses in the coloured variety. A light-coloured eye. Head narrow and elongated, or too short. Coat sparse, wavy or silky. Absence of the mane and "culotte". Coat too long, and white spots. Undershot or overshot mouth.

Note. — Male animals should have two apparently normal testicles fully descended into the scrotum.

MAIN AMERICAN KENNEL CLUB VARIATION TO STANDARD FOR THE SCHIPPERKE —

Weight. — Up to 18 pounds.

SCHIPPERKE REGISTRATIONS 1981 — 87 INCLUSIVE

1981 — 76
1982 — 95
1983 — 107
1984 — 82
1985 — 109
1986 — 84
1987 — 129

YET TO WIN CRUFTS BEST-IN-SHOW.

SCHNAUZER

The Schnauzer, sometimes known as the Standard Schnauzer, is a fine combination of good looks and toughness, the latter characteristic having been developed through a hard working past. Originating in the Wurttemberg and Bavaria regions of Germany in the early seventeenth century, he was used as a cattle drover, ratter and small game huner. Among his main ancestors is the Wire-haired German Pinscher which would account for the Schnauzer's Terrier-like qualities, 'Pinscher' translating roughly to 'Terrier'.

As Germany became more industrialised, so the need for the Schnauzer's working expertise dwindled. Instead he was put to good use as a guard dog in the towns and latterly he became a successful show breed. Shortly after his first show bench appearance in 1879 a standard was arrived at and his future was secured.

It was over twenty years later that the Schnauzer reached the U.S.A. and a further twenty until the British saw their first specimens. There is a liking for cropping the ears in the U.S.A., a practice banned in Britain.

Although not as popular as the smallest of the three types of Schnauzer, the Miniature, this breed is of a commendable disposition and is reliable in the home. The guarding of property, children or anything in his charge is second nature and he also has a great facility for play. Plenty of vigorous exercise is recommended and he will enjoy the challenge of being trained for specific tasks.

KEY TO CHARACTER	
INTELLIGENCE	****
TEMPERAMENT	****
EASE OF COAT CARE	**
SUITABILITY FOR SMALL DWELLING	***
***** (5) = VERY GOOD	

BRITISH KENNEL CLUB STANDARD

SCHNAUZER

GENERAL APPEARANCE. — The Schnauzer is a powerfully built, robust, sinewy, nearly square dog (length of body equal to height at shoulders). His temperament combines high spirits, reliability, strength, endurance and vigour. Expression keen and attitude alert. Correct conformation is of more importance than colour or other purely "beauty" points.

Head and Skull. — Head strong and elongated, gradually narrowing from the ears to the eyes and thence forward toward the tip of the nose. Upper part of the head (occiput to the base of the forehead) moderately broad between the ears — with flat, creaseless, forehead and well muscled, but not too strongly developed cheeks. Medium stop to accentuate prominent eyebrows. The powerful muzzle formed by the upper and lower jaws (base of forehead to the tip of the nose) should end in a moderately blunt line, with bristly, stubby moustache and chin whiskers. Ridge of the nose straight and running almost parallel to the extension of the forehead. The nose is black and full. Lips tight and not overlapping.

Eyes. — Medium sized, dark, oval, set forward, with arched bushy eyebrows.

Ears. — Neat and V shaped, set high and dropping forward to temple.

Mouth. — Scissor teeth, slightly overlapping from the top; with strongly developed fangs; healthy and pure white.

Neck. — Moderately long, nape strong and slightly arched, skin close to throat, neck set cleanly on shoulders.

Forequarters. — Shoulders flat and sloping. Forelegs straight veiwed from any position. Muscles smooth and lithe rather than prominent; bone strong, straight and carried well down to the feet; elbows set close to the body and pointing directly backward.

Body. — Chest moderately broad, deep, with visible strong breast bone reaching down to at least the height of elbow and slightly rising backward to loins. Back strong and straight, slightly higher at the shoulder than at the hindquarters, with short, well developed loins. Ribs well sprung. Length of body equal to height from top of withers to ground.

Hindquarters. — Thighs slanting and flat, but strongly muscled. Hindlegs (upper and lower thighs) at first vertical to the stifle, from stifle to hock, in line with the extension of the upper neck line, from hock, vertical to ground.

Feet. — Short, round, extremely compact with close-arched toes, (cat's paws) dark nails and hard soles. The feet also deep or thickly padded, pointing forward.

Tail. — Set on and carried high, cut down to three joints.

Coat. — Hard and wiry and just short enough for smartness, clean on neck, shoulder, ears and skull, plenty of good hard hair on front legs. Good undercoat is essential.

Colour. — All pepper and salt colours in even proportions, or pure black.

Height. — The ideal height for bitches shall be 45.7 cm (18″) and for dogs 48.3 cm (19″). Any variation of more than 2.5 cm (1″) in these heights should be penalised.

Faults. — Too heavy or too light; too low or high on the leg. Head too heavy or round, creased forehead, sticking-out, or badly carried, ears; light eye, with yellow or light grey rings; strongly protruding cheek-bones; flabby throat skin; undershot or overshot jaw. Muzzle too pointed or too small. Back too long, sunken or roached; barrel-shaped ribs; slanting crupper; elbows turned out; heels turned in, hindpart overbuilt (too steep). Toes spread open; paws long and flat (hare). Coat too short and sleek, or too long, soft or curled. All white, spotty, tigered or red colours. Small white breast spot or markings is not a fault. Among other serious faults are cow-hocks, sunken pasterns, or any weakness of joint, bones or muscular development.

Note. — Male animals should have two apparently normal testicles fully descended into the scrotum.

MAIN AMERICAN KENNEL CLUB VARIATION TO STANDARD FOR THE SCHNAUZER —

Known as the Standard Schnauzer in the U.S.A.

Ears. — Evenly shaped, set high and carried erect when cropped.

Height. — Ideal height at the highest point of the shoulder blades, 18½ to 19½ inches for males and 17½ inches to 18½ inches for females.

MAIN AMERICAN KENNEL CLUB VARIATION TO STANDARD FOR THE GIANT SCHNAUZER —

Ears. — When cropped, identical in shape and length with pointed tips. They are in balance with the head and are not exaggerated in length. They are set high on the skull and carried perpendicularly at the inner edges with as little bell as possible along the other edges.

SCHNAUZER REGISTRATIONS 1981 — 87 INCLUSIVE

1981 — 98
1982 — 122
1983 — 153
1984 — 125
1985 — 167
1986 — 144
1987 — 195

YET TO WIN CRUFTS BEST-IN-SHOW.

SHIH TZU

The energetic little Shih Tzu is one of the several small flat-faced breeds that herald from the Far East. All of these breeds obviously have a common ancestry stretching back thousands of years, but details are very sketchy. It seems very possible, though that the Shih Tzu was produced by crossing the Pekingese with Tibetan dogs of the type kept by the Dalai Lama, the all-powerful religious leader of Tibet. Much mystique surrounded dogs of the East in those far ancient times, and Pekingese/Shih Tzu — type dogs were known as 'Lion Dogs' after a half dog and half lion creature in Chinese mythology.

So prized were these dogs that the Chinese and Tibetans refused to allow them out of the East and the first Shih Tzu specimens to reach Europe in the early part of this century, were probably taken illegally. Since the breed's official recognition in Britain in 1934, there has been a steadily growing interest here. All major dog shows feature a large Shih Tzu entry and he is a dog suited admirably to the show environment. He always looks keen to impress, has a cheeky extrovert nature and an exotic attractiveness.

The Shih Tzu is a sociable dog and an ideal family pet provided enough time is spent on daily maintenance of the luxurious coat. He likes the company of children and never misses an opportunity to play, this being undertaken with great gusto. He is quite a hardy little dog with a sturdy frame and he will enjoy moderate amounts of daily exercise.

KEY TO CHARACTER	
INTELLIGENCE	***
TEMPERAMENT	****
EASE OF COAT CARE	*
SUITABILITY FOR SMALL DWELLING	*****
***** (5) = VERY GOOD	

BRITISH KENNEL CLUB STANDARD

SHIH TZU

GENERAL APPEARANCE. — Very active, lively and alert, with a distinctly arrogant carriage. The Shih Tzu is neither a terrier nor a toy dog.

Head and Skull. — Head broad and round; wide between the eyes. Shock-headed with hair falling well over the eyes. Good beard and whiskers; the hair growing upwards on the nose gives a distinctly chrysanthemum-like effect. Muzzle square and short, but not wrinkled like a Pekingese; flat and hairy. Nose black for preference and about one inch from tip to stop.

Eyes. — Large, dark and round but not prominent.

Ears. — Large, with long leathers, and carried drooping. Set slightly below the crown of the skull; so heavily coated that they appear to blend with the hair of the neck.

Mouth. — Level or slightly underhung.

Forequarters. — Legs short and muscular with ample bone. The legs should look massive on account of the wealth of hair.

Body. — Body between withers and root of tail should be longer than height at withers; well-coupled and sturdy; chest broad and deep, shoulders firm, back level.

Hindquarters. — Legs short and muscular with ample bone. They should look straight when viewed from the rear. Thighs well-round and muscular. Legs should look massive on account of the wealth of hair.

Feet. — Firm and well-padded. They should look big on account of the wealth of hair.

Tail. — Heavily plumed and curled well over back; carried gaily, set on high.

Coat. — Long and dense, but not curly, with good undercoat.

Colour. — All colours permissible, but a white blaze on the forehead and a white tip to the tail are highly prized. Dogs with liver markings may have dark liver noses and slightly lighter eyes. Pigmentation on muzzle as unbroken as possible.

Weight and Size. — 4.5 to 8.2 kg (10 to 18 lbs). Ideal weight 4.5 to 7.3 kg (10 to 16 lbs). Height at withers not more than 26.7 cm (10½″); type and breed characteristics of the utmost importance and on no account to be sacrificed to size alone.

Faults. — Narrow heads, pig-jaws, snipyness, pale pink noses and eye-rims, small or light eyes, legginess, sparse coats.

Note. — Male animals should have two apparently normal testicles fully descended into the scrotum.

MAIN AMERICAN KENNEL CLUB VARIATION TO STANDARD FOR THE SHIH TZU —

Size. — Height at withers 9 to 19½ inches, should be no more than 11 inches nor less than 8 inches. Weight of mature dogs 12 to 15 pounds, should be no more than 18 pounds nor less than 9 pounds.

SHIH TZU REGISTRATIONS 1981 — 87 INCLUSIVE

1981 — 1528
1982 — 1397
1983 — 1425
1984 — 1531
1985 — 1576
1986 — 1532
1987 — 1743

YET TO WIN CRUFTS BEST-IN-SHOW.

TIBETAN SPANIEL

Often mistaken for the shorter-faced Pekingese by the layman, the Tibetan Spaniel has unclear beginnings like most of the breeds from the east.

There is record of similar dogs being kept by the Tibetan monks for hundreds of years. Apparently the dogs would perform the quaint practice of turning their master's prayer wheels for them and this was probably still a common sight up until Tibet was invaded by the Chinese.

Although the Tibetan Spaniel, Pekingese, Tibetan Terrier and Lhasa Apso are all almost certainly related, it is not certain which of these breeds is the oldest. Any statements concerning the Tibetan Spaniel's early ancestry would be pure conjecture.

In 1958 the Tibetan Spaniel Association was formed in Britain and this perky, intelligent breed has experienced a steady if not meteoric rise in popularity. He is renowned as a first class show dog, being of convenient size, outgoing yet inoffensive nature and striking appearance when well groomed.

In the home he is safe in the company of small children and he will enjoy plenty of playful romps and regular walks, although his exercise needs are not excessive. Although slow to accept strangers, the Tibetan Spaniel is basically a sociable and commendable small dog.

KEY TO CHARACTER	
INTELLIGENCE	****
TEMPERAMENT	****
EASE OF COAT CARE	**
SUITABILITY FOR SMALL DWELLING	*****
***** (5) = VERY GOOD	

BRITISH KENNEL CLUB STANDARD

TIBETAN SPANIEL

CHARACTERISTICS. — Gay and assertive, highly intelligent, aloof with strangers.

GENERAL APPEARANCE. — Should be small, active and alert. The outline should give a well balanced appearance, slightly longer in body than height at withers.

Head and Skull. — Small in proportion to body and proudly carried giving an impression of quality. Masculine in dogs but free from coarseness. Skull slightly domed, moderate width and length. Stop slight, but defined. Medium length of muzzle, blunt with cushioning, free from wrinkle. The chin should show some depth and width. Nose black preferred.

Eyes. — Dark brown in colour, oval in shape, bright and expressive, of medium size set fairly well apart but forward looking giving an ape-like expression. Eye rims black.

Ears. — Medium size, pendant, well feathered in the adult and set fairly high. They may have a slight lift from the skull, but should not fly. Large heavy low set ears are not typical.

Mouth. — Ideally slightly undershot, the upper incisors fitting neatly inside and touching the lower incisors. Teeth should be evenly placed and the lower jaw wide between the canine tusks. Full dentition desired. A level mouth is permissible providing there is sufficient width and depth of chin to preserve the blunt appearance of muzzle. Teeth must not show when mouth is closed.

Neck. — Moderately short, strong and well set on. Covered with a mane or "shawl" of longer hair which is more pronounced in dogs than bitches.

Forequarters. — The bones of the forelegs slightly bowed but firm at shoulder. Moderate bone. Shoulder well placed.

Body. — Slightly longer from point of shoulder to root of tail than the height at withers, well ribbed with good depth, level back.

Hindquarters. — Well made and strong, hocks well let down and straight when viewed from behind. Stifle well developed, showing moderate angulation.

Feet. — Harefooted, small and neat with feathering between toes often extending beyond the feet. White markings allowed.

Gait. — Quick moving, straight, free, positive.

Tail. — Set high, richly plumed and carried in a gay curl over the back when moving. Should not be penalised for dropping tail when standing.

Coat. — Double coat, silky in texture, smooth on face and front of legs, of moderate length on body, but lying rather flat. Ears and back of forelegs nicely feathered, tail and buttocks well furnished with longer hair. Should not be over-coated and bitches tend to carry less coat and mane than dogs.

Colour. — All colours and mixture of colours allowed.

Weight and Size. — 4.1 to 6.8 kg (9 to 15 lbs) being ideal. Height about 25.4 cm (10″).

Faults. — Large full eyes, broad flat muzzle, very domed or flat wide skull, accentuated stop, pointed weak or wrinkled muzzle, overshot mouth, long plain down face without stop, very bowed or loose front, straight stifle, cow hocks, nervousness, cat feet, coarseness of type, mean expression, liver or putty coloured pigmentation, light eyes, protruding tongue.

Note. — Male animals should have two apparently normal testicles fully descended into the scrotum.

TIBETAN SPANIEL REGISTRATIONS 1981 — 87 INCLUSIVE

1981 — 430
1982 — 445
1983 — 493
1984 — 517
1985 — 462
1986 — 444
1987 — 400

YET TO WIN CRUFTS BEST-IN-SHOW.

TIBETAN TERRIER

The Tibetan Terrier is in fact not a true Terrier at all, such a name being given to dogs that burrow underground to locate game or vermin. Although this activity does not feature in the history of the Tibetan Terrier, his is still a working past.

In his homeland of Tibet he was known for thousands of years as the 'holy dog' and like most Tibetan breeds his early development was probably in the monastries. But he led a more rugged life than the other more pampered breeds and was used widely as a sheepdog and even in a guarding role. Although he was a more practically employed dog than, for instance the Tibetan Spaniel, he was still a breed that the Tibetans guarded jelously.

But eventually specimens did reach Europe. In Britain, it was very unclear at first as to what exactly constituted a Tibetan Terrier. Early dogs were known as Lhasa Terriers and some bore resemblance to the Shih Tzu or the Lhasa Apso and some were more like the modern Tibetan Terrier. It was not until the 1930's that the Tibetan Breeds Association was formed in a concerted effort to sort things out.

Since his proper classification, he has won a fair size following here and features quite strongly in the show world. Looking a little like a scaled-down Old English Sheepdog, he has a marvellous outgoing nature and strong prescence. His greatest physical asset is his coat which is stunning if properly prepared.

His guarding instinct is used to full effect in the home but that is normally the only aggression the Tibetan Terrier will show. He is full of fun and will enjoy plenty of exercise and play sessions.

KEY TO CHARACTER	
INTELLIGENCE	***
TEMPERAMENT	****
EASE OF COAT CARE	**
SUITABILITY FOR SMALL DWELLING	***
***** (5) = VERY GOOD	

BRITISH KENNEL CLUB STANDARD

TIBETAN TERRIER

CHARACTERISTICS. — Alert, intelligent and game, not fierce nor pugnacious. Chary of strangers.

GENERAL APPEARANCE. — A well muscled medium sized dog, in general appearance not unlike an Old English Sheepdog in miniature.

Head and Skull. — Skull of medium length, not broad or coarse, narrowing slightly from ear to eye, not domed but not absolutely flat between the ears. The malar bones are curved, but should not be over developed so as to bulge. There should be a marked stop in front of the eyes, but this must not be exaggerated. The head should be well furnished with long hair, falling forward over the eyes. The lower jaw should carry a small, but not exaggerated amount of beard. The length from eye to tip of nose equal to length from eye to base of skull; not broad nor massive. Nose black.

Eyes. — Large, dark, neither prominent nor sunken: should be set fairly wide apart. Eyelids dark.

Ears. — Pendent, not too close to head, V shaped, not too large, heavily feathered.

Mouth. — Level by preference but if slightly undershot not to be penalised.

Forequaters. — Legs parallel and heavily furnished. Pasterns slightly sloping.

Body. — Compact and powerful. Length from point of shoulder to root of tail equal to height at withers. Well ribbed up. Loin slightly arched.

Hindquarters. — Heavily furnished, should be slightly longer than forelegs with well bent stifles and low set hocks giving a level back.

Feet. — The feet should be large, round, heavily furnished with hair between the toes and pads. The dog should stand well down on its pads. There should be no arch in the feet.

Gait. — When walking or trotting the hind legs should neither go inside nor outside the front ones but run on the same track.

Tail. — Medium length, set on fairly high and carried in a gay curl over the back. Very well feathered. There is often a kink near the tip.

Coat. — Double coated. The undercoat fine wool, the top coat profuse, fine but not silky or woolly; long; either straight or waved.

Colour. — White, golden, cream, grey or smoke, black, particolour, and tri-colours; in fact any colour except chocolate or liver colour.

Size. — Height at shoulders, dogs should be from 35.6 to 40.6 cm (14 to 16″), bitches slightly smaller.

Faults. — ·A weak snipy foreface should be penalised. Lack of double coat, Cat feet.

Note. — Male animals should have two apparently normal testicles fully descended into the scrotum.

MAIN AMERICAN KENNEL CLUB VARIATION TO STANDARD FOR THE TIBETAN TERRIER —

Weight and Size. — Average weight 22 to 23 pounds, but may be 18 to 30 pounds.

TIBETAN TERRIER REGISTRATIONS 1981 — 87 INCLUSIVE

1981 — 404
1982 — 411
1983 — 571
1984 — 522
1985 — 601
1986 — 662
1987 — 625

YET TO WIN CRUFTS BEST-IN-SHOW.